MASSACHUSETTS

The Bay State

★

TEN TOP FACTS ABOUT MASSACHUSETTS

★ ★ ★ ★ ★ ★ ★ ★ ★ ★ ★ ★ ★

•State nicknames:	The Bay State, Old Colony State
•State motto:	*Ense petit placidam sub libertate quietem* (By the sword we seek peace, but peace only under liberty.)
•Capital:	Boston
•Area:	8,262 square miles
•State flower:	Mayflower
•State tree:	American elm
•State bird:	Chickadee
•State dog	Boston terrier
•State drink:	Cranberry juice
•State dessert:	Boston cream pie

With love to some of my favorite Bay State natives: Mom, Dad, Carol, Craig, Jeffrey, and Robert, and, as always, to Brian, Moses, and Jacob.

p. 4: U.S. Mint; p. 5: (bottom left and right) North Wind Picture Archives, Alfred, ME; p. 6 (both) North Wind Picture Archives; p. 7: (all) North Wind Picture Archives; p. 8: (both) North Wind Picture Archives; p. 9: (top left) North Wind Picture Archives, (bottom) Superstock Images, Jacksonville, FL; p.10: (top) North Wind Picture Archives; p. 11: (all) North Wind Picture Archives; p. 12: North Wind Picture Archives; p. 13: (both) Corbis; p. 14: Superstock Images; p. 15: (top left) Superstock Images, (bottom) Dorothy Wilding/John F. Kennedy Library and Museum, Boston, MA; p. 16: Corbis; p. 17: Superstock Images; p. 18: (top left) Kindra Clineff Photography, Winchester, MA (top right) Corbis, (bottom right) Kindra Clineff; p. 19: (left top and bottom) Superstock Images, (right) Corbis; p. 20: (top left) North Wind Picture Archives, (all others) Kindra Clineff; p. 21: (top left and bottom right) Kindra Clineff, (top right) N. Carter/North Wind Picture Archives; p. 22: (all) Superstock Images; p. 23: Pacha/Bettmann/Corbis, New York, NY (Damon, Affleck), Robert Frost Library, Amherst College, Amherst, MA (Dickinson), Bettmann/Corbis (Du Bois); p. 24: Superstock Images (Emerson), Bettmann/Corbis (Geisel), North Wind Picture Archives (Revere), Bettmann/Corbis (Wheatley); p. 25: Bettmann/Corbis.

Photo research by Dwayne Howard

All other illustrations by John Speirs

No part of this publication may be reproduced in whole or in part, or stored in a retrieval system, or transmitted in any form or by any means, electronic, mechanical, photocopying, recording, or otherwise, without written permission of the publisher. For information regarding permission, write to Scholastic Inc., Attention: Permissions Department, 555 Broadway, New York, NY 10012.

ISBN 0-439-22281-8

Copyright © 2001 by Scholastic Inc.

Published by Scholastic Inc. SCHOLASTIC and associated logos are trademarks and/or registered trademarks of Scholastic Inc. All rights reserved.

The Official 50 State Quarters Club is a publication of Scholastic Inc. that has been developed in conjunction with The Jim Henson Company under a license from the United States Mint. 50 State Quarters logo, and the official Treasury Department/United States Mint seal are trademarks of the United States Mint. JIM HENSON is a trademark of The Jim Henson Company. All rights reserved.

THE Jim Henson COMPANY

12 11 10 9 8 7 6 5 4 3 2 1   1 2 3 4 5 6/0

Designed by Madalina Stefan

Printed in the U.S.A.

First Scholastic printing, February 2001

Scholastic has a wide range of fun, high-quality book clubs for children of all ages. Please visit our Web site at www.scholastic.com/athomeclubs.

MASSACHUSETTS

The Bay State

By Alexandra Hanson-Harding

SCHOLASTIC INC.
New York Toronto London Auckland Sydney Mexico City New Delhi Hong Kong

A Celebration of the Fifty States

★ ★ ★ ★ ★ ★ ★ ★ ★ ★ ★ ★

In January 1999, the U.S. Mint started an ambitious ten-year program to commemorate each of the fifty United States. Over the next several years (through 2008), they will issue five newly designed quarters each year.

One side (obverse) of each new quarter will display the profile of George Washington and the words *Liberty, In God We Trust,* and *United States of America.* The other side (reverse) will feature a design honoring a specific state's unique history, the year it became a state, the year of the quarter's issue, and the words *E Pluribus Unum* (Latin for "from many, one"). The quarters are being issued in the order in which the states joined the union, beginning with the thirteen original colonies.

To find out more about the 50 State Quarters™ Program, visit the official U.S. Mint Web site at *www.usmint.gov.*

MASSACHUSETTS' QUARTER: Ready at a Minute's Notice

The Massachusetts quarter depicts "The Minuteman," a statue in the Minuteman National Historical Park in Concord by Daniel Chester French, the same sculptor who made the statue of Abraham Lincoln that sits in the Lincoln Memorial. The original Minutemen were farmers and townsmen who trained as soldiers so they could fight the British during the Revolutionary War. Always at the ready, they were prepared to assemble and fight on short notice, which is how they got their name. Their courage helped to change the future of the continent.

The outline of the state behind the statue on the quarter's reverse side shows why Massachusetts is called the Bay State—because of the huge bay encircled by the Massachusetts mainland and Cape Cod (the long curve of land on the right).

The *Mayflower*

The First Settlers in the New World

As with all the original colonies, the land that is now Massachusetts was first occupied by many different Indian tribes. For several thousand years before the Europeans arrived, these tribes lived side by side, sometimes at peace, sometimes at war. Adventurous Europeans explored Massachusetts for centuries before the colony was settled. Tragically, the diseases they brought to the New World wiped out much of the Indian population in the early 1600s.

On September 16, 1620, a small ship called the *Mayflower* left England for the "New World." On board, the Pilgrims, as they would later be called, were Separatists, members of a strict religious group that wanted to worship in their own way, not in the way of the official Church of England. After a harsh sixty-six-day voyage, they settled at a place they called Plymouth (named after an English city) on December 21, 1620, starting the first English colony north of Virginia.

Native American greeting the *Mayflower*

Pilgrims building their settlement at Plymouth

The first Thanksgiving

The going was rough for the Pilgrims. Only about half the colonists survived the first winter. Wampanoag Indians who lived nearby showed them how to use fish as fertilizer for corn and taught them to hunt for deer and other game. In gratitude, after their first bountiful harvest, the Pilgrims invited the Wampanoag for a three-day feast in 1621—the first Thanksgiving.

Over the next few years, many members of a religious sect, called the Puritans, arrived and settled in the area. But Massachusetts really began to grow in 1630, when a ship called the *Arbella* brought one thousand Puritans to the state. They had been given a charter by England's king to start the Massachusetts Bay Company. With this charter, the Puritans founded Boston (now the capital of Massachusetts), and other settlements including Charlestown, Springfield, Northampton, and Salem. Troubles under England's King Charles I soon forced thousands of other Puritans to flee their country, and by 1640, more than ten thousand settlers lived in Massachusetts.

The Puritans were hardworking and strong believers in education. Although they wanted religious freedom for themselves, they were not always willing to give it to others. Quakers, Baptists, and members of other faiths were driven out of the state or otherwise punished for their beliefs. One of those driven out was Roger Williams, a Baptist leader who went on to found Rhode Island. Another was Anne Hutchinson, a Puritan who was punished for leading church services because she was a woman.

Boston in the 1660s

War and Witches

The settlers and the Indians lived peacefully together for many years, but in 1675, war broke out between a Wampanoag leader called King Philip and the settlers. The settlers were taking up more and more of his people's land, and King Philip wanted to drive the settlers away. It was a long and bloody war and several hundred people on both sides were killed. In 1676, the settlers won and the Indians were driven off their land.

King Philip

Indian raid on settlers in King Philip's War

Witch trial in Salem

A few years later, another tragic chapter in Massachusetts's history took place: the Salem witch trials. Many seventeenth-century Puritans believed witchcraft was the work of the devil and that it caused sickness and death. When a group of young girls claimed that some of their neighbors had put evil spells on them, some community leaders believed them. No one knows for sure what caused the girls to make their accusations; however, the more attention they got, the more people the girls accused. The results were deadly. One hundred fifty people were imprisoned as witches in Salem and twenty people were executed. When it was over, people were ashamed of having taken part in the event; it had been like a contagious disease that swept over the town, contaminating neighbor after neighbor.

Colonial Days and the Fight for Independence

In the year 1700, Boston was the biggest city in the colonies. Massachusetts slowly became less religious and more commercial, developing into a center for building ships, manufacturing shoes and guns, as well as becoming a center for trading. As time went on, the people of Massachusetts became consumed over what to do about the colony's ties to England. England spent a lot of money fighting a war called the French and Indian War (1754–1763) on behalf of the colonies, and tried to pass along the cost to the colonists by taxing them. The colonists lacked fair legal representation in Britain's Parliament and were outraged at being made to pay taxes on which they couldn't vote. Before long, they began to feel that they were not really British at all.

In 1764, a crowd gathered at Boston's Faneuil Hall to protest these taxes, but nothing changed. In fact, the next year the British Parliament passed the Stamp Act, which forced the colonists to pay taxes on all legal documents, licenses, commercial contracts, newspapers, pamphlets, and playing cards. The British also tried to force the colonists to buy goods only from them, even if the price was unfairly high. Then they imposed higher taxes on these goods, enraging the colonists. Realizing that the colonists were becoming uneasy under their rule, the British stationed troops in Boston to keep the protesters under control.

The Boston Massacre

In 1770, British soldiers fired on the crowd at another protest, killing five people, including a runaway slave and patriot named Crispus Attucks. This event, known as the Boston Massacre, inflamed the colonists even more. On December 16, 1773, one hundred men disguised as Indians dumped more than two hundred crates of tea into Boston Harbor. They did it to protest a British monopoly on tea, another overpriced commodity they could only buy from England. In response to the Boston Tea Party, Britain's Parliament passed what came to be

The Boston Tea Party

Paul Revere's midnight ride

known as the "Intolerable Acts," laws restricting freedom in Massachusetts. Tensions grew even higher, and on April 18, 1775, it looked as if British troops would soon attack. Patriot and silversmith Paul Revere made his famous midnight ride from Boston to Concord to warn all who could hear him, "The British are coming." The next morning the Revolutionary War began with a shot fired in Lexington, "the shot heard 'round the world." It marked the beginning of the Siege of Boston. In June 1775, one of the first battles of the war took place in Massachusetts: the Battle of Bunker Hill. The British lost one thousand soldiers before the colonial militiamen ran out of gunpowder, allowing the enemy to take over a small fortification on nearby Breed's Hill. The British occupied Boston for months.

It wasn't until March 17, 1776 that General George Washington freed Boston. British troops fled the city and didn't return. More than 80,000 Massachusetts soldiers fought bravely during the war, which ended in 1783. Five years later, George Washington revisited Boston as the first President of the United States.

After the war ended, Massachusetts became the sixth state to ratify the Constitution on February 6, 1788. Massachusetts leader John Adams became the first Vice President of the United States and its second President. Later, John Quincy Adams, his son, would become the sixth President.

George Washington watches the raising of the first American flag in Boston in 1776.

Workers at one of Lowell's textile mills

From Farm to Factory

The nineteenth century was a time of great creativity and change in Massachusetts. In 1810, a businessman named Francis Cabot Lowell went to England to study the methods and machinery used to make clothes. When he returned a few years later, he set up the first fabric-making factory in the United States, and the Industrial Revolution in Massachusetts began. Soon, huge water-powered textile mills were built in what became the town of Lowell, and thousands of New England farm girls were employed there. By the 1850s, paper, firearms, shoes, and other goods were also manufactured in Massachusetts's cities. Many farmers began to leave the countryside, either to move west for better land, or to find higher wages in the state's rapidly growing industrial centers.

At first, factory workers were treated well. But after a while, as competition increased, their wages dropped and living conditions grew worse. The workers banded together and formed unions to go on strike for decent wages.

A Time of Awakening

The air in Massachusetts seemed to be full of ideas. Some of America's greatest writers of the 1800s lived near one another in eastern Massachusetts—writers such as Ralph Waldo Emerson, Henry David Thoreau, Nathaniel Hawthorne, and Louisa May Alcott. In the town of Amherst in the northwestern part of the state, a reserved young woman named Emily Dickinson wrote intense, brilliant poems in solitude, most of them undiscovered until after her death. Herman Melville wrote his great epic, *Moby-Dick,* in nearby Pittsfield.

Henry David Thoreau

Nathaniel Hawthorne

Many Massachusetts intellectuals were becoming increasingly concerned about human rights. Early feminists such as Lucy Stone, who refused to change her name when she married, began to petition for women's rights. Later, Massachusetts native Susan B. Anthony would follow in her footsteps. Dorothea Dix started working to improve conditions in prisons and in asylums for the mentally ill. Horace Mann introduced the idea of universal public education. In 1829, William Lloyd Garrison began speaking against slavery at the Park Street Church in Boston. He also started an antislavery newspaper in Boston called *The Liberator.* He worked to help free slaves and convinced many Bostonians to join the cause. Massachusetts became a refuge to thousands of slaves and a major stop on the Underground Railroad.

William Lloyd Garrison

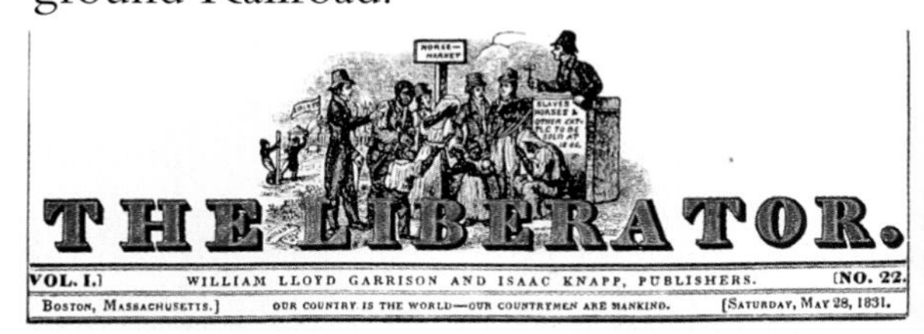

THE LIBERATOR.

VOL. I.] WILLIAM LLOYD GARRISON AND ISAAC KNAPP, PUBLISHERS. [NO. 22.

BOSTON, MASSACHUSETTS.] OUR COUNTRY IS THE WORLD—OUR COUNTRYMEN ARE MANKIND. [SATURDAY, MAY 28, 1831.

Masthead of Garrison's abolitionist newspaper

A Flood of Immigrants

Many immigrants from countries all over Europe came to Massachusetts during the nineteenth century, drawn by the industrial opportunities there. Irish people in particular began to flood the state in the middle of the century after a terrible famine in their homeland left many starving. Although they were welcomed at first, soon their overwhelming numbers and their sick condition made them unwanted. They faced severe prejudice. Some shops posted signs that said, "Irish Need Not Apply," meaning they refused to hire any Irish immigrants. It would take time before they became part of the social fabric of the state, but eventually the Irish became leaders in business, politics, and cultural life.

Attack on Fort Wagner by soldiers of the 54th Massachusetts Regiment

Civil War

The concern over immigrants faded into the background when it became clear that a war between the Southern and Northern United States was about to begin. When the Southern states seceded and formed a new nation, President Abraham Lincoln declared war. More than 1,500 men from Massachusetts quickly joined the Union army. Among Massachusetts's greatest Civil War heroes were the Union army's 54th Massachusetts Volunteer Infantry Regiment. These brave soldiers were among the first units of African-American soldiers from a free state. They were tough fighters who proved themselves in an 1863 battle at South Carolina's Fort Wagner. Almost three hundred of the approximately 1,600 men in the 54th Regiment were killed or wounded in the battle. One of the soldiers, William H. Carney, became the first African-American to receive the Congressional Medal of Honor for his bravery in that battle.

Striking workers

A New Century

After the war, Massachusetts continued to be an important industrial center. Before long, though, times grew hard for the immigrant laborers who worked long hours in the factories for low wages in unsafe conditions. In January 1912, more than 20,000 impoverished workers in Lawrence went on strike. When police were called in to keep order, fights broke out. Finally, after two months, workers and factory owners reached a compromise and the strike ended.

In 1919, the Boston police went on

The Boston police strike

strike for better wages and the right to form a union. The state's governor, Calvin Coolidge, called out the National Guard

Calvin Coolidge

to end the strike, saying, "There is no right to strike against the public safety by anybody, anywhere, anytime." This move made him famous nationwide and the next year he ran and won as Vice President under Warren Harding. In 1923, he became President after Harding died, and was elected to office in 1924.

During the early to mid-1920s, workers continued to lose their jobs as textile companies moved out of Massachusetts to build new factories in the South, where labor was cheaper. The state was one of the first to feel the effects of the Great Depression, which began in 1929 and lasted until the start of World War II.

Once the war started, the U.S. military relied on the large number of educated men and women who graduated from Massachusetts's colleges. Massachusetts led the way in developing new defense technology used during the war. In addition, the first U.S. jet engines were built in Massachusetts, and workers made much-needed supplies and weapons in the state's factories.

When the war ended in 1945, Massachusetts continued to be at the forefront of scientific research. Physicists and engineers from Harvard University and the Massachusetts Institute of Technology (MIT) helped the country plunge into the space race with the Soviet Union.

The space program was still going strong in 1960, when Massachusetts Senator and Harvard graduate John F. Kennedy ran for President. Despite widespread prejudice against Catholics at that time, he won and became the youngest man ever to be elected to the White House. Tragically, President Kennedy was assassinated in 1963 during his third year in office. He was one of the most popular Presidents of all time. During his term he started the Peace Corps, a volunteer agency of Americans sent overseas to help less-developed countries, introduced important civil rights legislation, sent the first Americans into space, and improved relations with the Soviet Union.

John F. Kennedy

The Kennedys of Massachusetts

In 1919, when Rose Fitzgerald, daughter of one of Boston's mayors, married Joseph Kennedy, a wealthy banker and son of a prominent local politician, they combined two important political families. Several of their nine children eventually became involved in politics and ran for public office. Today, many of their thirty grandchildren and more than fifty great-grandchildren have gone on to hold important positions in government, journalism, and the arts.

The Kennedy family has frequently been touched by scandal and tragedy. Among the tragedies were the assassinations of John and Robert (John's younger brother, who was campaigning for the presidency) and the 1999 death of John F. Kennedy Jr. in a plane crash. In spite of these events, the close-knit family has created a remarkable legacy.

The family of Joseph and Rose Kennedy

Massachusetts Today

Massachusetts is still an important industrial center. Its factories produce equipment used in the textile, printing, and paper industries in addition to sophisticated high-technology products. And for a small state, a lot of farming is done in Massachusetts. It is famous for its delicious, crisp MacIntosh apples, and produces half of all the cranberries consumed in the United States. Fishing is also a major industry—shrimp, lobster, flounder, scallops, and of course, cod, all come from Massachusetts.

Boston is Massachusetts's largest city and its capital. Its modern skyscrapers tower over tiny, curved streets that were cow paths in colonial times. Every April 17, thousands of runners from all over the world come to compete in the grueling Boston Marathon, a twenty-six-mile race that goes from the town of Hopkington into Boston. It is America's oldest annual long-distance race.

In addition to the dozens of colleges and universities in Boston—not to mention the nation's first university, Harvard, located in nearby Cambridge—Massachusetts is home to many other prestigious schools of higher education, including Williams College, Amherst College, the University of Massachusetts, Smith College, Mount Holyoke College, Tufts University, and Brandeis University.

The Boston Marathon

The state has nearly 120 public and private colleges.

Millions of visitors come to the state every year, drawn by its history, culture, and natural beauty. Some of the country's finest museums are located in Massachusetts, including the Isabella Stewart Gardner Museum, housed in a Venetian-style palazzo in Boston. The sandy beaches of Cape Cod are world-famous summer vacation spots, while the picturesque Berkshire hills in the west attract vacationing skiers in the winter. The state is dotted with quaint little towns with village greens and white-spired churches. Along with the other five states in the region called New England, the Massachusetts countryside is famous for its spectacular fall foliage.

Talk Like a Bostonian:

Boston is known for its unique accent. R's are dropped when they appear at the end of a word or in the middle of a word before a consonant. R's are added to words that end in vowels. The city also has its own special lingo. Here are a few examples:
•**Spa:** small convenience store •**Packie:** package store •**Grinder:** submarine sandwich •**Tonic:** soda •**Hamburg:** hamburger •**Frappe:** milk shake

Boston Harbor today

Things to Do, Places to See

Display at the Basketball Hall of Fame

Basketball Hall of Fame

In 1891, a teacher named James Naismith invented basketball while trying to think of an indoor sport to keep his students active in the winter. He put up peach baskets at the two ends of a gym and had players try to toss balls into them. Now, the 48,000-square-foot Basketball Hall of Fame is located in Springfield, the city where the game was invented. At the Hall of Fame, visitors can see a movie in a wraparound movie theater, shoot baskets, and check out more than two hundred basketball heroes who are honored there.

The Berkshires

The beautiful Berkshire hills rise in the western part of the state and draw tourists all year round. Visitors come for skiing in the winter; hiking in the spring; swimming, vacationing, and cultural events such as the Tanglewood Music Festival in Lenox and Jacob's Pillow Dance Festival in Lee in the summer; and foliage viewing in the fall.

Autumn in Massachusetts

The Berkshires were once home to artist Norman Rockwell and writer Edith Wharton, and visitors can see the Norman Rockwell Museum in Stockbridge and take tours of Wharton's home, The Mount, in Lenox. Also open for tours is a house called Arrowhead in the town of Pittsfield, where Herman Melville wrote his famous novel *Moby-Dick*. The Hancock Shaker Village in Pittsfield shows how the Shakers, a small religious sect, lived in the nineteenth century.

Norman Rockwell's studio in Stockbridge

Cape Cod National Seashore

The Cape and Islands

Well-known for their spectacular, unspoiled beaches and dramatic seascapes, millions of people come each summer to visit Cape Cod and the islands of Martha's Vineyard and Nantucket. On the cape, visitors can sightsee or window-shop in quiet seaside towns, relax on the wide sandy beaches, and walk around busy Provincetown, an artists' colony famous for its shops, art galleries, and restaurants. There's also the forty-mile-long Cape Cod National Seashore, a preserved coastal area great for hiking, biking, and bird-watching.

The main town on the island of Nantucket, also called Nantucket, was once one of the whaling capitals of the world. A whaling museum in the town explains what it was like to work in this dangerous industry and displays harpoons and other whaling tools.

Martha's Vineyard

Martha's Vineyard was named even before the Pilgrims came to Massachusetts. Benjamin Gosnold, who was surveying the land for the English in 1602, named it after his daughter, Martha. He was also the man who named Cape Cod for all the fish he saw there.

Fenway Park

The most famous of Massachusetts's sports teams is the Boston Red Sox, who play in Fenway Park. Built in 1912, the stadium is the smallest and oldest of America's major league ballparks. The first major league series was played in Boston in 1903, but the Red Sox haven't won a World Series since 1918. Some people say the Red Sox are suffering the "Curse of the Bambino." That year, baseball great Babe Ruth was traded from the Red Sox to the New York Yankees. The park is also associated with many other baseball legends, such as Ty Cobb, Shoeless Joe Jackson, Ted Williams, and Carl Yasztremski.

Home of the Boston Red Sox

Boston's State House

Freedom Trail

One of Boston's leading attractions is the Freedom Trail. Visitors can follow a two-and-a-half-mile trail through the heart of Boston to see some of its most important historical sights. It starts at Boston Common, America's oldest public park, and goes past Boston's State House, the Old Granary burying ground (where many famous Bostonians are buried), and Faneuil Hall, a Revolutionary War meeting place that is called the "Cradle of Liberty." It also leads visitors to Paul Revere's house, the ship "Old Ironsides," and Bunker Hill, site of a Revolutionary War battle.

Textile mill in Lowell National Historical Park

Lowell National Historical Park

The Lowell National Historical Park is a complex of buildings, barges, and trolleys that help to tell the story of how the Industrial Revolution began in America. More than 750,000 visitors come here each year to see the 1820s water-powered textile factories, the quarters where mill workers once lived, and to learn about the rise, fall, and rebirth of industry in the northeastern United States. Boat rides through the canals that once powered the mills afford visitors a closer look at the mills' inner workings. You can even punch a time card, put in earplugs, and go into the noisy weave room where young women once worked fourteen-hour days.

Corn husking at Old Sturbridge Village

Old Sturbridge Village

This central Massachusetts attraction, located about midway between the cities of Worcester and Springfield, is a re-creation of a typical New England town in the early 1800s. You can see costumed interpreters make cider in a horse-powered cider mill, sew shoes, hammer out barrels, or run a water-powered sawmill. Some of the animals are "back-bred"—bred to be just like the species that people in 1830 would have owned.

Pilgrim village at Plimoth Plantation

Plimoth Plantation

This living-history museum depicts life as it was in the Plymouth Colony in 1627. It has old houses with thatched roofs, native plants, and seventeenth-century herbs. Surrounding the cottages are fields of corn and rye and grazing sheep. The interpreters dress and act like the people who lived at the original Plimoth Plantation. Near the plantation, visitors can see Plymouth Rock, where the Pilgrims first set foot in America, and take a tour of the *Mayflower II,* a re-creation of the original *Mayflower.*

Salem

This seafaring town has a long history, but it is best known for one of its most infamous happenings: the 1692 Salem witch trials, when dozens of people were falsely imprisoned for being witches. There are four separate museums in Salem with exhibits about the trials. Visitors also come to see the historic Custom House Maritime Museum, Pioneer Village (a re-creation of a 1630 Puritan village), and the House of Seven Gables, made famous by a book of the same name by Nathaniel Hawthorne.

Stone wall memorial to victims of witch hunt in Salem

Walden Pond

This pond is only half a square mile in size, but it plays a big role in history. Henry David Thoreau, a Massachusetts author, spent several years at Walden Pond. He built his own cabin along its banks to spend time in solitude thinking, writing, and observing nature. He wrote a famous book, *Walden,* about his experience living alone by the pond. Visitors can go to Walden Pond today, but the spot has changed immeasurably since Thoreau's day. Now it is a park where thousands come each weekend to swim and sunbathe.

Walden Pond

Famous People from Massachusetts

John Adams (1735–1826)

John Adams, born in the town of Braintree (now called Quincy), started out as a country lawyer and grew to become one of our nation's great leaders. In 1774, he became one of Massachusetts's representatives to the Continental Congress in Philadelphia. A few years later, he helped to create the Declaration of Independence. In 1777, after the Revolutionary War began, he went to France and later the Netherlands to gain their help in the war. When he returned to the United States, he was elected Vice President under George Washington. On March 4, 1797, he became the second President of the United States and the first to live in the White House. He lost his second election in a bitter contest with Thomas Jefferson. Eventually, he and Jefferson became friends again and both died on July 4, 1826, fifty years to the day after the signing of the Declaration.

Susan B. Anthony (1820–1906)

Susan B. Anthony was born to a Quaker family in 1820 in the town of Adams. When she grew up and became a teacher, she became involved in the antislavery movement. As time went on, she and her friend Elizabeth Cady Stanton also began to petition for women's rights. She fought for women teachers to get the same pay as men, for women to be allowed to enter universities, and most important, for women to gain the right to vote. She was a leader in the women's suffrage movement for more than fifty years. Her dream of winning the right to vote for women never came true during her lifetime, but fourteen years after her death, the Nineteenth Amendment to the Constitution was ratified, finally granting women this right. On July 2, 1979, the U.S. Mint honored her work by issuing the Susan B. Anthony dollar coin.

Clara Barton (1821–1912)

This schoolteacher from Oxford obtained and distributed much-needed supplies to soldiers during the Civil War. In 1865, when the war ended, she got the idea—and permission from President Abraham Lincoln—to start the Bureau of Records to trace missing soldiers. While living in Switzerland, she helped establish hospitals to treat soldiers wounded during the Franco-Prussian War. When she returned to the United States, she started the American Red Cross and served as its first president from 1882 to 1904. She devoted the rest of her life to traveling all over the world, supervising relief efforts during wars and natural disasters.

Matt Damon (1970–) and Ben Affleck (1972–)

These two movie stars are real-life best friends who grew up in Cambridge, where they attended the same school. In addition to acting in some of the same movies, they have written screenplays together. Although they both started acting before they were ten, they hit the big time when they moved to Hollywood in their twenties. Among the movies they have appeared in together are *Good Will Hunting* (which they cowrote and won an Academy Award for the screenplay in 1998), *Chasing Amy,* and *Dogma.*

Emily Dickinson (1830–1886)

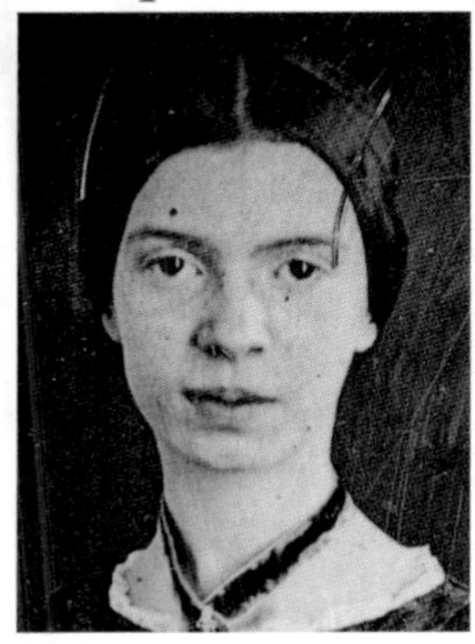

Poet Emily Dickinson grew up in the small town of Amherst. She had a normal childhood in many ways, and even had a year of college at Mt. Holyoke. But once she returned home, she became reclusive. She almost never went out and saw no visitors other than close family members. Dickinson corresponded by mail with her many friends, including her sister-in-law, who lived right next door! She spent much of her solitary time writing, and she produced over 1,700 poems, only ten of which were published while she was alive. Her powerful, deeply original verses have made her reputation as one of America's greatest poets.

William Edward Burghardt (W.E.B.) Du Bois (1868–1963)

W.E.B. Du Bois was born in Great Barrington, in the Berkshire hills, and had a happy childhood. But when he won a scholarship to Fisk University in Nashville, Tennessee, he experienced severe discrimination for the first time and saw how his fellow African-Americans were mistreated in the South. He later attended Harvard University, where he was the first black man to receive a doctoral degree from the school. He was a brilliant scholar who wrote many articles and books, including his masterpiece, *The Souls of Black Folk.* Most of his writings protested the prejudice African-Americans faced. He helped to found the National Association for the Advancement of Colored People (NAACP) in 1909, and for many years edited its newspaper, *The Crisis.*

Ralph Waldo Emerson (1803–1882)

Ralph Waldo Emerson was born in Boston and lived in Concord. Trained as a minister, he quit his post because of differences with the church and devoted his life to speaking and writing. This original thinker developed a new philosophy called transcendentalism. Many people considered him a radical as he spoke out against materialism and in favor of individual freedom and love of nature. Over time, the ideas he expressed in poems, essays, and lectures have entered America's mainstream.

Theodor Geisel (Dr. Seuss) (1904–1991)

This Springfield native, using the pen name Dr. Seuss, wrote and illustrated many great children's classics such as *The Cat in the Hat* and *Green Eggs and Ham.* Before he became a children's book creator, he worked in advertising for fifteen years and made Oscar-winning documentaries for the U.S. Army during World War II. But his works for children brought him a special kind of fame. His first book, *It Happened on Mulberry Street,* presents an imaginative view of life in his hometown of Springfield. He went on to write forty-six other books, all of which have sold millions of copies and have been translated into dozens of languages.

Paul Revere (1735–1818)

Patriot and silversmith Paul Revere was born in Boston. He created the state seal of Massachusetts and designed the first paper money to be used in the colonies. Revere believed strongly in independence from the British and took part in the Boston Tea Party. But he is most famous for his midnight ride on horseback on the eve of the Revolutionary War. On the night of April 18, 1775, along with William Dawes and Samuel Prescott, he rode from Boston to Concord to warn residents that British troops were advancing. Paul Revere was actually stopped by the British, but Samuel Prescott got through to the colonists in time.

Phillis Wheatley (1753?–1784)

Brought to the New World as a slave, Phillis Wheatley was educated by her owners in Boston, who recognized her great intelligence. She began writing poems when she was thirteen, and became America's first important African-American poet.

Little Women

Although born in Pennsylvania in 1832, Louisa May Alcott spent most of her life in Massachusetts. She exhibited writing talent from an early age, and after working as a teacher and a housekeeper, Alcott began writing to relieve her family's financial worries.

In addition to her writing, which included mysteries, poems, thrillers, and stories for children, Louisa May Alcott served as a nurse during the Civil War and later joined the campaign for women's suffrage. Her female characters were usually depicted as strong, self-reliant, and imaginative women. Based on recollections of her own childhood, her novel Little Women *(1868) describes the differing personalities and fortunes of four sisters. In the following excerpt, Jo March (Alcott's literary alter ego) has just received a copy of the newspaper containing her first published story, "The Rival Painter." After sharing it with Laurie, the boy next door, she surprises her family with the news of its publication and delights in the prospect of being able to help support them.*

With a loud "Hem" and a long breath, Jo began to read very fast. The girls listened with interest, for the tale was romantic, and somewhat pathetic, as most of the characters died in the end.

"Who wrote it?" asked Beth, who had caught a glimpse of Jo's face.

The reader suddenly sat up, cast away the paper, displaying a flushed countenance, and, with a funny mixture of solemnity and excitement, replied in a loud voice, "Your sister."

"You?" cried Meg, dropping her work.

"It's very good," said Amy, critically.

"I knew it! I knew it! Oh, my Jo, I am so proud!" and Beth began to hug her sister, and exult over this splendid success.

"Tell us all about it."

"When did it come?"

"How much did you get for it?"

"What will Father say?"

"Won't Laurie laugh?" cried the family, all in one breath, as they clustered about Jo; for these foolish, affectionate people made a jubilee of every little household joy.

"Stop jabbering, girls, and I'll tell you everything," said Jo, wondering if Miss Burney felt any grander over her *Evelina,* than she did over her *Rival Painters.* Having told how she disposed of her tales, Jo added, "And when I went to get my answer, the man said he liked them both, but didn't pay beginners, only let them print in his paper, and noticed the stories. It was good practice, he said; and when the beginners improved, anyone would pay. So I let him have the two stories, and today this was sent to me, and Laurie caught me with it, and insisted on seeing it, so I let him; and he said it was good, and I shall write more, and he's going to get the next paid for, and I *am* so happy, for in time I may be able to support myself and help the girls."

Jo's breath gave out here; and, wrapping her head in the paper, she bedewed her little story with a few natural tears; for to be independent, and earn the praise of those she loved, were the dearest wishes of her heart, and this seemed to be the first step towards that happy end.

A Recipe from Massachusetts, Land of the Cranberry

The cranberry bogs of Plymouth County in eastern Massachusetts produce half of the nation's cranberries. In fact, at the Cranberry World Visitors Center in Plymouth you can see how cranberries are grown and harvested. You can even visit the cranberry bogs. Here's a recipe for delicious cranberry muffins, a Massachusetts favorite. Make sure to have an adult help you.

Cranberry Muffins

Ingredients:

- $1\frac{1}{2}$ cups all-purpose flour
- $\frac{1}{2}$ cup sugar
- 2 teaspoons baking powder
- $\frac{1}{2}$ teaspoon salt
- 1 egg, lightly beaten
- $\frac{1}{2}$ cup milk
- $\frac{1}{4}$ cup vegetable oil
- $\frac{3}{4}$ cup fresh cranberries

Preheat the oven to 400°F. Combine the flour, sugar, baking powder, and salt in a large bowl. Combine the egg, milk, and oil in a small bowl. Make a well in the center of the dry mixture and pour in the liquid mixture, stirring just until moistened. Fold the cranberries into the batter. Spoon into greased or paper-lined muffin tins, filling each cup two-thirds full. Bake for 20 to 25 minutes. Remove the muffins from pans immediately. Makes 12 muffins.